14 Days of

Self Love

a Self-Paced Workbook

from

SOBER Relationship Blueprint ®

Create a self-loving mindset, raise your self-esteem & be brave enough to pursue your goals.

in omnia paratus
publishing

www.inomniaparatuspublishing.com

Welcome

Your Self-Love Journey Starts Here

Hello,

I created this self-paced workbook when I noticed that many women continue to be self-sacrificing and overcompensating because they may feel that 'everyone else's needs are more important' than their own or maybe they don't think that they have any 'worth'.

I know that this is how I used to think and feel too.

When I created & did the exercises in this workbook, I started to learn more about myself and I came to know in my heart that I AM worthy and capable of self-love. - I KNOW that you are too!

I wanted to share my SOBER Relationship Blueprint® exercises to get you started on your journey by creating a brand-new self-loving mindset for yourself.

Enjoy YOUR Journey!
YOU are Worth It!

Warmly,
Louie B
Founder
Sober Relationship Blueprint ®

14 Thinking Traps

Which of these 14 Thinking Traps are keeping you from having healthy self-esteem?
Tick the circles that apply to you 70% of the time.

1. CATASTROPHIZING

Assuming the worst possible outcome automatically. Making things seem more dire than they actually are.

2. 'ALL OR NOTHING' THINKING

Black-and-white thinking. Thinking in extremes. Ex: "If I don't get a job at a top company, I'm a complete failure. It's 'do or die'."

3. OVER-GENERALIZING

Making sweeping statements based on one negative incident. Ex: "All bosses are out to take advantage of their employees - just like my current boss."

4. NEGATIVE FILTER

Focusing on the negative aspects of something/ignoring its positive qualities. Ex: "Everything about me is bad. I look bad, I have no confidence, I have no education and a low-paying job."

5. JUMPING TO CONCLUSIONS

Making negative inferences and drawing conclusions without checking the facts. Ex: Assuming that your colleague is plagiarizing your work without asking him or her directly or investigating the matter.

6. MIND-READING

Assuming that you know what other people are feeling or thinking with no facts to back up your assumptions.

7. EMOTIONAL REASONING

Using emotions to make judgments. Ex."I feel so stupid making that mistake, so I must be a stupid person."

14 Thinking Traps (cont)

Which of these 14 Thinking Traps are keeping you from having healthy self-esteem?
Tick the circles that apply to you 70% of the time

8. MUSTS / SHOULDS

Being rigid by believing that you 'should' or 'must' be/do something. Ex. You 'should' be in a specific job or that you 'must' get married by a certain age or you will be a failure .

9. LABELING

Describing a person or something using a general label based on 1 characteristic. Ex: Labeling a person (or yourself) as an 'idiot' because of 1 mistake.

10. BLAMING

Taking responsibility/taking the blame for negative events even when it is not your fault. Or blaming others when it is your fault.

11. CHANGE FALLACY

The belief that other people or circumstances should change to make you happy.

12. CONTROL FALLACY

Believing that we are powerless or taking the 'victim' role when something unwanted happens.

13. FAIRNESS FALLACY

Unrealistically expecting everything in the world to be fair, then getting upset when things are not 'fair' in our eyes.

14. REWARD FALLACY

Expecting a reward after self-sacrificing & feeling resentment when there is no reward at the end of your sacrifices.

SOBER
Relationship Blueprint

Do You Notice Yourself Thinking 'Unhelpful Thoughts'?

STEP 1

WHAT IS THE SITUATION MAKING YOU FEEL UNCOMFORTABLE?

STEP 2

WHAT WERE YOU DOING?

STEP 3

WHAT WERE YOU TELLING YOURSELF?

STEP 4

HOW DID YOU FEEL?

STEP 5

WHAT THOUGHTS FLASHED THROUGH YOUR MIND?

Keep a Diary of these 'Unhelpful Thoughts' (ex)

THE 'PROBLEM' (add these details) Who were you with? What were you doing? When did it happen?	YOUR FEELINGS What did you feel? <1 word> How intense was it on a scale of 0-100%?	CATCHING YOUR THOUGHTS What flashed through your mind? What bad things might happen? What does it say about me? Which Thinking Trap is this?
I failed an interview for a job that I really wanted.	Disappointed - 80% Feeling worthless -80% Embarrassed - 60%	I will NEVER get a job I want. - 90% I will be jobless and worthless for a long time - 70% I am lousy & have no useful skills. - 80% **Thinking traps: Catastrophizing, over-generalizing**

Thoughts Diary (cont)

THE 'PROBLEM' (add these details) Who were you with? What were you doing? When did it happen?	YOUR FEELINGS What did you feel? <1 word> How intense was it on a scale of 0-100%?	CATCHING YOUR THOUGHTS What flashed through your mind? What bad things might happen? What does it say about me? Which Thinking Trap is this?

Thought-Challenging Diary

Get rid of your self-critical thoughts & be brave enough to pursue your goals

Let's Dig Deeper (ex)

My self-critical thought: "I'm a failure. I give up easily & not had success with many activities I start. This project will be the same."

EVIDENCE SUPPORTING THIS SELF-CRITICAL THOUGHT

I was excited to start a coaching business last year and hired someone to design my website. But I lost interest after that.

I also gave up when it became difficult to get clients. Wasted my money designing a website. Felt dsappointed in myself.

EVIDENCE AGAINST THIS SELF-CRITICAL THOUGHT

I did not give up 'easily'. It took me 2 months to let this business idea go.

I did not do a proper market research to see if my type of coaching service had a demand. That was why it was difficult to get clients.

NEW EVIDENCE-BASED THOUGHT

I'm not a failure - I was simply too excited and did not do market research before launching my coaching business.

I have learned that I need to do research properly and start small. There is no need to hire an expensive website designer in the beginning stages of launching a business.

WHAT DO YOU FEEL NOW AFTER INSTALLING A NEW THOUGHT?

Before this exercise:
-embarrassed
-disappointed in myself
-guilty

Now:
-assured
-more confident
-motivated

Thought-Challenging Diary

My self-critical thought:

_____

EVIDENCE SUPPORTING THIS SELF-CRITICAL THOUGHT	EVIDENCE AGAINST THIS SELF-CRITICAL THOUGHT
NEW EVIDENCE-BASED THOUGHT	**WHAT DO YOU FEEL NOW AFTER INSTALLING A NEW THOUGHT?**

Let's Work On Change
Track the Following

IDENTIFY PROBLEM	UNHELPFUL COPING STRATEGIES	WHAT WOULD BE A MORE HELPFUL COPING STRATEGY?
PAGE NO. 1		
MON		
TUES		
WED		
THURS		
FRI		
SAT		
SUN		

Success Log

What are the big & small successes you've achieved this week?

Week of:

Date:

Date:

Date:

Date:

Date:

Date:

Date:

Date:

Date:

You Are Worthy

1. Which 'I'm Not Good Enough' thoughts are prevalent in your mind?

(ex: "I'm a failure because I'm not running a successful business like my friend Sarah.")

2. When you were growing up, which adult in your life kept saying that you were not 'good enough'?

(Why do you think she/he/they said that? Why was she/he/they so bent on you being 'perfect' or 'successful?)

3. How did you feel when those words were said to you?

(ex: hurt, disappointed, heartbreaking, sad)

You Are Worthy (cont)

4. Write 3 ways how low self-esteem and confidence have stopped you from doing what you want?

(ex: "I did not create videos for my business because I don't have confidence in front of the camera")

5. Write 2-3 ways how self-criticism has helped you.

(ex: "Self-criticism pushed me to work harder and produce good quality work.")

6. How does your behavior change when your mind criticizes you? List 3 ways.

(ex: "I shrink & become unsure of myself." "I follow what everyone else is doing & end up unhappy.")

You Are Worthy (cont)

7. Now that you notice your self-criticism, what are some things you can do to boost your self-worth?

(ex: "I will continue doing what I'm good at: making videos for an audience." "I will plan for more small successes every week." "Choose to hang out with people who make me feel good for the way I am.")

8. Recall a moment when you felt full of confidence and joy. What were you doing + who helped you get there?

(ex: "I felt full of self-worth when my coaching client told me that she felt good about herself after seeing me." "I felt full of self-worth when my good friends told me I have a talent for cooking.")

9. List down the names of 3 people whose lives are better and/or made easier because of you. Why?

Should You Keep Or Change Your Beliefs & Decisions? (ex)

Advantages of
keeping my perfectionist attitude at work

My work will be high quality, have little mistakes and my reputation as a hard worker will remain intact.

3 Emotions I'll Feel: satisfied, proud, secure

Advantages of
changing my perfectionistic attitude at work

I will enjoy my life more. I will have more energy to spend with my kids, my partner, and/or friends. I will also be able to sleep better at night.

3 Emotions I'll Feel: relaxed, happier, less anxious

Disadvantages of
keeping my perfectionist attitude at work

My relationships with my kids, partner, friends may suffer as my mental energy is dedicated to my work most of the time.

3 Emotions I'll Feel: anxious, highly stressed out, guilty

Disadvantages of
changing my perfectionistic attitude at work

I think my work will suffer. The quality will dip. I don't like feeling as though I did not give my 100% in my projects. I hate submitting shoddy work.

3 Emotions I'll Feel: anxious, embarrassed, shame

Keep or Change Your Beliefs & Decisions?

Advantages of

_____

3 Emotions I'll Feel:

Advantages of

_____

3 Emotions I'll Feel:

Disadvantages of

_____

3 Emotions I'll Feel:

Disadvantages of

_____

3 Emotions I'll Feel:

Face Your Flaws the Self-Loving Way (ex)

What are the 1-3 'weaknesses' which impact my life? (sample)	What strategies can I apply? Using these 3 *Face Your Flaws* mentioned below, pinpoint which strategy to adopt + create 1 action plan for each 'weakness'
1. Being too hard on myself	**Strategy/lies:** "Be kinder to yourself" **Action plan:** From tomorrow on, I will set a to-do list that is very manageable. If I can't finish any task today, I will let it roll over to the following day. It's okay if I can't finish every task today - just focus on the crucial ones.
2. Being a perfectionist	**Strategy/lies:** "Design a unique system to work around your 'weaknesses' " **Action plan:** I will delegate 1 household chore to my partner from tomorrow on. He/She/They may not do it as perfectly as I wish, but I willl accept it anyway so I won't get stressed over chores everyday!
3. Procrastinating	**Strategy/lies:** "Design a unique system to work around your 'weaknesses' " **Action plan:** To be more disciplined, I will plan my day tomorrow. I will allocate 60 minutes for every task on my list. This will push me to work fast without expecting perfection.

Face your Flaws the Self-Loving Way (cont)

What are the 1-3 'weaknesses' which impact my life?	What strategies can I apply? Using these 3 *Face Your Flaws* mentioned below, pinpoint which strategy to adopt + create 1 action plan for each 'weakness'
1.	**Strategy/lies:** **Action plan:**
2.	**Strategy/lies:** **Action plan:**
3.	**Strategy/lies:** **Action plan:**

Your Personal Strengths Decoded

To raise our self-esteem, we need to examine our strengths.
What are your skills? What do you know a lot about? What valuable work experience do you have? What are you gifted in? What are your positive qualities?
If you can't think of any, ask a friend or family member for their perspective.

Your Skills	Your Knowledge	Your Experience	Your Abilities + Talents	Your Positive Qualities

7-Steps for
Successful Problem Solving (ex)

1. PINPOINT THE PROBLEM

I procrastinate and plan too much.
I want to create an effective 30-day online course. But I know it is going to take a lot of time and energy. I am overwhelmed by the planning that I will need to do. Every time I think of working on my online course, I get anxious.

2. LIST DOWN ALL THE POSSIBLE SOLUTIONS

- Pay a graphic designer to design the course worksheets & materials for me.
- Create a shorter course (maybe a 7-day or 14-day course) that is manageable for me to create and manageable for my students to follow through.
- Don't create an online course at all.

3. LIST THE PROS AND CONS OF EVERY POSSIBLE SOLUTION

- **Hire a graphic designer** - I will have more time to create videos & worksheets for my clients. However, I don't have the cashflow to hire someone
- **Create a shorter course** - I can complete a short course without overwhelm, but will it compromise the quality?
- **Don't create an online course at all** - More time for me to create videos, which I enjoy! However, this keeps me stuck where I am & I don't grow.

7-Steps for
Successful Problem Solving (ex /cont)

4. PICK THE ONE SOLUTION WHICH MAKES YOU FEEL RELIEVED

Rank the solutions in order of preference:
- Create a shorter course
- Don't create an online course
- Hire a graphic designer

I am choosing to create a shorter course.
I will create a power-packed course - giving my clients results fast

5. PLAN HOW YOU ARE GOING TO IMPLEMENT THE SOLUTION. WHAT ACTIONS ARE YOU GOING TO TAKE?

I will draw a mindmap on a big sheet of paper to plan my course-creation process.
I will create 2 course materials every day - beginning tomorrow morning at 10am.
I will finish creating the online course by (insert date).

6. TAKE ACTION IMMEDIATELY. WRITE THE TIMELINES OF WHEN YOU ARE GOING TO START IMPLEMENTING THE ACTIONS ABOVE.

I will take a big sheet of paper & start sketching my online course.
I will allow myself 2 weeks to complete this.
I will sign up for an online platform to host my online courses.
(I will start creating the first lesson tomorrow morning at 10am. No excuses!

7-Steps for Successful Problem Solving (ex /cont)

7. AFTER TAKING ACTION, REVIEW THE SOLUTION AFTER A REASONABLE TIME. DOES IT WORK WELL?

It turns out that allocating only 2 weeks to create an online course is not enough for me.

I have 2 other freelance jobs and a 3 year old toddler to manage. After some reflection, I realized that my perfectionism is also slowing me down.

IF IT DOES NOT WORK WELL, WHAT DO YOU THINK IS THE CAUSE? LOOKING FORWARD, REPEAT STEPS 4-7. (BE FLEXIBLE WHEN NEEDED)

I will stick to my choice, but I will modify my plans.
I will give myself an extra week to finish creating my online course. My new deadline will be (insert date) instead of (insert previous deadline)
I will also be disciplined to follow my schedule. I will not let my perfectionism slow my progress. I can't create perfectly beautiful course materials and that is okay.

NOTES + REFLECTIONS
WHAT HAVE I LEARNED?

7-Steps for
Successful Problem Solving.

1. PINPOINT THE PROBLEM

2. LIST DOWN ALL THE POSSIBLE SOLUTIONS

3. LIST DOWN THE PROS AND CONS OF EVERY POSSIBLE SOLUTION

7-Steps for
Successful Problem Solving.

4. PICK THE ONE SOLUTION WHICH MAKES YOU FEEL RELIEVED

5. PLAN HOW YOU ARE GOING TO IMPLEMENT THE SOLUTION. WHAT ACTIONS ARE YOU GOING TO TAKE?

6. TAKE ACTION IMMEDIATELY. WRITE THE TIMELINES OF WHEN YOU ARE GOING TO START IMPLEMENTING THE ACTIONS ABOVE.

7-Steps for
Successful Problem Solving

7. AFTER TAKING ACTION, REVIEW THE SOLUTION AFTER A REASONABLE TIME. DOES IT WORK WELL?

IF IT DOES NOT WORK WELL, WHAT DO YOU THINK IS THE CAUSE? LOOKING FORWARD, REPEAT STEPS 4-7. (BUT BE FLEXIBLE WHEN NEEDED)

**NOTES + REFLECTIONS
WHAT HAVE I LEARNED?**

date: _____

My 10 Emotional States (ex)

Track the 10 emotions YOU feel on a typical, uneventful day.
Put a (*) in the box for positive emotions and an (X) in the box for the negative emotions.

(sample emotions)

Motivated	*
High-Energy	*
Passionate	*
Confident	*
Anxious	X
Stressed	X
Excited	*
Curious	*
Joyful	*
Irritated	X

date: _____

My 10 Emotional States (ex)

**Track the 10 emotions YOU feel on a typical, uneventful day.
Put a (*) in the box for positive emotions and an (X) in the box for the negative
emotions.**

_____	☐
_____	☐
_____	☐
_____	☐
_____	☐
_____	☐
_____	☐
_____	☐
_____	☐
_____	☐

The Bravery Ladder

Experts recommend 'graded exposure' which means, experiencing your stressful situations one baby step at a time.

Example:

Let's say someone has a fear of public speaking.

Let's see how we can use 'graded exposure' using The Bravery Ladder method.

Ask the person to write her/his/their LEAST FEARED activity at Level 1 leading all the way up to the MOST FEARED activity at Level 6 (which may be public speaking).

Using
The Bravery Ladder

Sample Bravery Ladder

LEVEL 6: Most feared activity
Public speaking

LEVEL 5
Creating a 'live' video on Facebook
or Instagram Stories

LEVEL 4
Giving feedback to a waiter
or chef at a restaurant

LEVEL 3
Presenting to a group of 2-3 friends

LEVEL 2
Giving a presentation in front
of another person

LEVEL 1: Least feared activity
Speaking in front of the mirror

Using
The Bravery Ladder (cont)

The person can experience the Level 1 activity (which is, speaking in front of the mirror) first for 4-5 times a week.

Or until her/his/their anxiety about that Level 1 activity reduces to about 50%. Whichever comes first.

Then s/he/they will move on to the Level 2 activity (which is giving a presentation in front of another person).

Similarly, s/he/they will do this 4-5 times a week or until her/his/their anxiety for this Level 2 activity dies down by 50%. Whichever comes first.

This will go on until s/he/they reach(es) Level 6

My Bravery Ladder

My Bravery Ladder

LEVEL 6: My most feared activity

LEVEL 5

LEVEL 4

LEVEL 3

LEVEL 2

LEVEL 1

Be Fearless

Stop Caring What Other People Think - Pursue Your Goals Now

Fill In the Below Boxes

1. **What are you actually afraid of?**

2. **What is the worst that can happen?**

3. **What are 3 things I can do to prevent the 'worst' from happening?**

4. **Do you expect perfection from the beginning?**

Be Fearless

Stop Caring What Other People Think - Pursue Your Goals Now

5. What would you do if I told you that you will flop the first few times?

6. What do you feel if I told you that you will get it right (after some time)?

7. What is one tiny step you can do to put yourself closer to your goal?

8. What is the second tiny step?

Be Fearless

Stop Caring What Other People Think - Pursue Your Goals Now

9. When will you start the first step?

10. When will you start the second step?

Saying 'Yes'
When I Mean 'No'
Fill In the Below Boxes

1. When I say "Yes" during the times I don't want to do something, I feel :

2. When I say "Yes" I want other people to think I am :

Maybe you want people to like you, think you're kind, nice, reliable, hard-working, helpful or you want to make yourself indispensable?

3. By saying "Yes", what am I saying "No" to in my own life?

Whenever we say "Yes" to something, we're saying "No" to something else - even if that something is simply relaxing at home (self-care is important!).

4. When I say "No" to other people's requests, I feel :

Saying 'Yes'
When I Mean 'No'

5. When I say "No" I worry other people will think I am :

6. If I said "No", I could say "Yes" to these things in my life

7. My biggest fears about saying "No" are :

NOTES + REFLECTIONS
WHAT HAVE I LEARNED?

Eliminate Envy

Fill In the Below Boxes

What do I envy about
_____ ?

What do I have that (person's name)
_____ may be envious of?

What problems might _____ be
facing that I don't know about?

What does my envy show about
what I want in my life?

Hurt & Healing for Self-Love

Fill In the Below Boxes

The trigger I felt:

How _____ (fill in trigger person's name) should act in my ideal world:

How I felt when _____ performed the 'trigger':

My automatic belief when _____ performed the 'trigger':

Hurt & Healing for Self-Love

Is this belief realistic? Why/why not?

Is this belief helpful for me? Why/why not?

What are the possible reasons _____ acted ike that?

How will/can I handle this trigger next time?

Congratulations

You've Completed Your
14-Day
Self-Love Journey!

Your self-love journey does not end here - You are just beginning this wonderful growth & You Are Worthy!

We learn we grow, and we learn some more.

And through it all, we will learn to love ourselves.

Embrace and love all of yourself - past, present, and future.

Self-love will take hold and become a guiding force in your life.

If you have any questions/comments about this 14-Day Self Love Course, DM me on Instagram: instagram.com/sober_relationship_blueprint/.

Warmly,
Louie B
Founder
SOBER Relationship Blueprint®